CH

D1121523

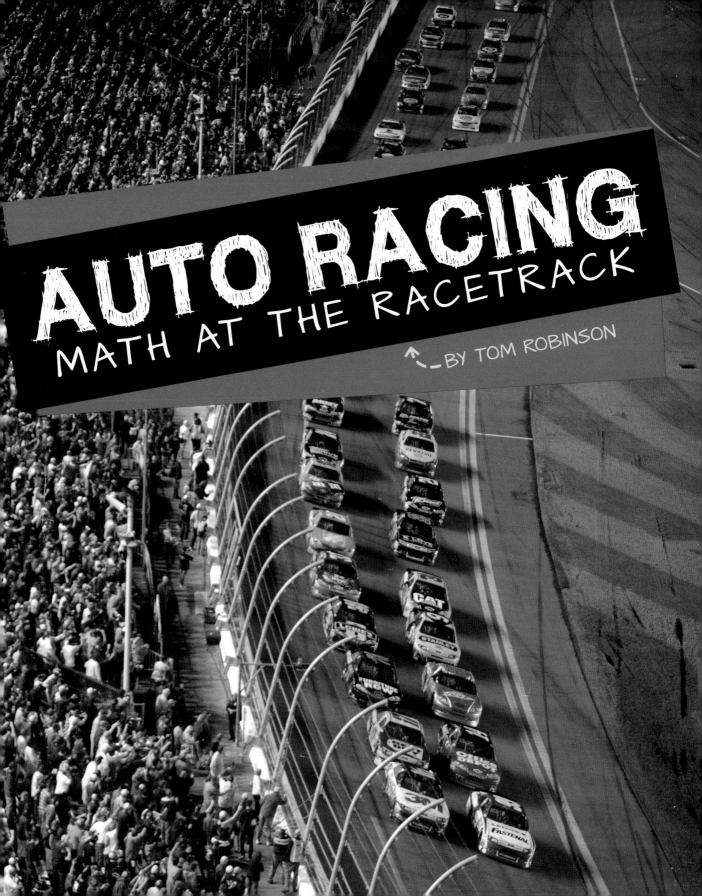

AUTO RACING
MATH AT THE RACETRACK

BY TOM ROBINSON

The Child's World®

Published by The Child's World®
1980 Lookout Drive • Mankato, MN 56003-1705
800-599-READ • www.childsworld.com

Acknowledgments
The Child's World®: Mary Berendes, Publishing Director
The Design Lab: Design and production
Red Line Editorial: Editorial direction

Photographs ©: Phelan M. Ebenhack/AP Images, Cover,
Title; Photo Works/Shutterstock Images, 4, 22–23; Walter
G Arce/Shutterstock Images, 6–7; ISC Archives/Getty
Images, 8–9; Cal Sports Media/AP Images, 10–11; Mel
Evans/AP Images, 12–13; Shutterstock Images, 14–15;
Hodag Media/Shutterstock Images, 16; Rainier Ehrhardt/
AP Images, 18–19; Bruce Yeung/Shutterstock Images,
20–21; Doug James/Shutterstock Images, 24–25; Darron
Cummings/AP Images, 26–27; Beelde Photography/
Shutterstock Images, 29

ISBN 9781614734062
LCCN 2012946501

Printed in the United States of America
Mankato, MN
November, 2012
PA02144

ABOUT THE AUTHOR

Tom Robinson is the author of 33 books, including 25 about sports. The Susquehanna, Pennsylvania, native is an award-winning sportswriter and former newspaper sports editor.

TABLE OF CONTENTS

Mike Conway drives an open-wheel car during the IndyCar series Toyota Grand Prix on April 17, 2011.

MATH AT THE RACETRACK

At the racetrack, drivers race their cars against each other and the clock. Speed is measured in time and miles per hour (mph). It can also be measured in fractions of seconds spent on pit stops.

Math is used to explain many parts of auto racing. The track's length and the length of each race are both measured in miles. Car parts must meet certain measures as part of the rules.

Series of races often decide all-season champions. Formulas are used to find the number of points drivers receive in each race.

There are many numbers used in an auto race or racing season. Use your math skills as you take a look at auto racing. You'll be surprised at how much they are needed!

The Sport

The painted numbers and ads say one thing on a car—that it is meant for racing. Without them, the cars racing in the National Association for Stock Car Auto Racing (NASCAR) would look similar to those on the street. The cars, however, move at much faster speeds.

NASCAR is by far the largest stock car racing **organization** in the world. Stock car originally meant racing with a car that was built to be driven on the street. Stock cars have become much different, though. The cars in NASCAR are now built just for racing.

Auto racing comes in many forms. Different types of cars are used in different types of races. Stock car, open-wheel, and drag racing are all forms of racing. The styles are different, but the goal is the same. Each driver wants to be the first to cross the finish line.

Open-wheel cars have wheels that are outside the car body. Open-wheel cars are about half the weight of stock cars. They tend to race at higher speeds.

IndyCars are the most common in open-wheel racing in the United States. The Indianapolis 500 is the most famous race for IndyCars. Formula 1 is a major international series for open-wheel cars.

Ashley Force-Hood drives her Castrol GTX funny car during the 41st Annual Gatornationals on March 14, 2010.

Most NASCAR vehicles are heavier than other race cars. They can get into the range of 200 mph. But they usually are not as fast as other forms of race cars.

Drag racing is one quick burst down a **straightaway**. Many kinds of cars are used. One kind of car used in drag races is a funny car. Drag racers need to reach incredibly high speeds in seconds. Many can go faster than 300 mph in that short burst. A common distance for a drag race is a quarter of a mile.

How long is a quarter-mile race in yards? How about feet? To find this, divide the number of yards in a mile by four. That equals one-fourth of a mile. There are 1,760 yards in a mile.

$1,760 \div 4 = 440$
There are 440 yards in a quarter mile.

There are 3 feet in a yard. Multiply the yards by three.

$440 \times 3 = 1,320$
There are 1,320 feet in a quarter mile.

Track Styles

Drivers race their cars down a pair of 3,330-foot stretches at Indianapolis Motor Speedway. Each stretch leads into the turns at the famous oval track.

The tracks used for auto races come in various shapes and sizes. Many tracks have an oval shape. Oval tracks have two straightaways. They are usually connected by two 180° turns. A pair of 90° turns can also be joined by a shorter straight stretch.

Daytona International Speedway has a tri-oval track. This track has three sets of turns. The **frontstretch** is 3,800 feet. The **backstretch** is 3,000 feet.

Racetracks can be shorter than a mile. They can also be more than 2.5 miles, such as the 2.66-mile Talladega Superspeedway in Alabama.

Some tracks have a quad-oval shape. Others are D-shaped ovals. All the turns are to the left. Another setting for racing is a road course. This kind of course has a series of turns in each direction.

Talladega Superspeedway is a tri-oval racetrack.

2.66 MILES LONG

Two of the most famous American races share the names of their tracks. The Daytona 500 is a NASCAR event in Florida. The Indianapolis 500 is a famous race in the United States.

Both races are named for the number of miles they have. They are each 200 laps. How many miles are in each lap?

To determine the number of miles per lap, divide the total miles by the total laps.

500 ÷ 200 = 2.5 miles

Each lap at the Daytona and Indianapolis racetracks is 2.5 miles long.

BACKSTRETCH

FRONTSTRETCH

Track Measurements

NASCAR has short, **intermediate**, superspeedway, and road course tracks. NASCAR breaks down tracks by length. Short tracks are up to 1 mile. Intermediate tracks are 1 to 2 miles. Superspeedways are longer than 2 miles.

Richmond International Speedway is a short track. It is .75 miles long.

For shapes, NASCAR has different types of oval and road courses. Within those types there are differences in tracks. This table compares the seven D-shaped tracks that host NASCAR Sprint Cup races.

TRACK	LENGTH (MILES)	FRONTSTRETCH (FEET)	BACKSTRETCH (FEET)
Chicagoland Speedway	1.5	2,400	1,700
Fontana Auto Club Speedway	2.0	3,100	2,500
Kansas Speedway	1.5	2,685	2,207
Kentucky Speedway	1.5	1,662	1,600
Las Vegas Motor Speedway	1.5	3,330	3,330
Michigan International Speedway	2.0	3,600	2,242
Richmond International Raceway	.75	1,290	860

Cars have the greatest speed on straightaways. The longer straightaways and flatter tracks allow the fastest speeds. Michigan has a 3,600-foot straightaway. It has the fastest track records.

This 2011 NASCAR Sprint Cup series race is at the D-shaped track at Richmond International Raceway in Richmond, Virginia.

Dale Jarrett drove an **average** of 174 mph for an entire race at Michigan. Ryan Newman averaged 194.2 mph for a qualifying lap.

Fontana has the second-best set of times. As a wider track, it has more room in its corners for better **average** speeds over the course of an entire lap.

The slowest overall records are on the smallest track. Richmond's race record was set by Dale Jarrett's 109 mph. Its **qualifying** record was set by Brian Vickers at 130 mph.

Jimmie Johnson won the 2012 Brickyard 400 in 2 hours, 54 minutes, 19 seconds. Because 54 minutes is 9/10 of an hour, 2 hours 54 minutes equals 2.9 hours. What was his average speed?

400 miles ÷ 2.9 hours = 137.9 mph

His average speed was 137.9 mph.

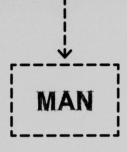

MAN

The Racing Team

A racing team is made of more than just a driver and car. There are people who work on the business of racing. And there are people who work on the cars. Mechanics get cars ready. Pit crews adjust cars during a race in what are called pit stops.

During a race, all work is done as quickly as possible to return the car to the track. Fuel is added, tires are changed, and urgent repairs are made.

NASCAR began an annual Sprint Pit Crew Challenge in 2005. For one day, pit crews from the top 24 teams become the center of attention. Crews compete to see which can complete a pit stop in the least amount of time.

Jimmie Johnson's crew won in 2012. Johnson's team was able to change four tires, put in gas, and push the car 40 yards in 22.239 seconds in the final. Teamwork and planning save time.

Figure out how much time a crew can save through teamwork. A crew might need 13.7 seconds to change tires, 9.2 seconds to refuel, and 9.5 seconds to push the car back onto pit road. Add the seconds together to find the total time.

13.7 + 9.2 + 9.5 = 32.4 seconds
It took 32.4 seconds to do the tasks separately.

Dale Earnhardt Jr.'s pit crew works on his car during a NASCAR Sprint Cup series race on August 5, 2012, at Pocono Raceway.

But the same team can complete the stop in 23.2 seconds total if all tasks are done at the same time. How many seconds does working at the same time save?

32.4 - 23.2 = 9.2 seconds
Done together, the tasks were done 9.2 seconds faster.

Mechanical Measures

A mechanic needs to tighten a bolt in an engine. It is important to match the wrench size to the object on which it is used. Mechanics use different sizes of tools. Gauges check tires for wear and how much air is in them. Other tools and computers look at how well the engine is working.

The wrenches that mechanics use are measured in fractions of inches. The fractions are fourths, eighths, sixteenths, and thirty-seconds.

A race car mechanic needs to find a wrench quickly. Imagine the mechanic needs to organize a set of wrenches by their sizes. Put the following wrenches in order from smallest to largest fractions of an inch:
$1/2$, $1/4$, $3/4$, $3/8$, $5/8$, $5/16$, $7/8$, $7/16$, $9/16$, $11/16$, $11/32$, $13/16$

To place in order, you first need to convert all of the fractions to a common **denominator**. All the wrench sizes measured can be changed to have a denominator of 32.

Convert $3/4$ to 32nds by multiplying the **numerator** and denominator by the same number.
$3/4 \times 8/8$

Multiply the numerators together.
$3 \times 8 = 24$

Then multiply the denominators together.
$4 \times 8 = 32$
The fraction is $24/32$.

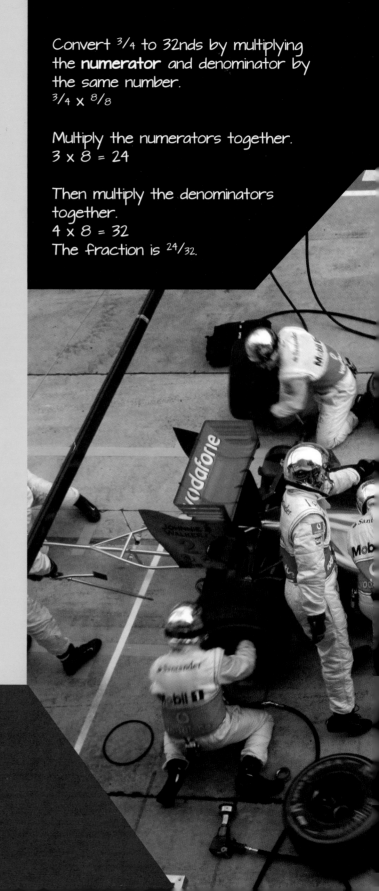

Mechanics rush to service Lewis Hamilton's car at a pit stop during the final race of the 2009 Formula 1 Petronas Malaysian Grand Prix.

Here are the wrench sizes with a denominator of 32.

$3/4 = 24/32$
$1/2 = 16/32$
$1/4 = 8/32$
$3/4 = 24/32$
$3/8 = 12/32$
$5/8 = 20/32$
$5/16 = 10/32$
$7/8 = 28/32$
$7/16 = 14/32$
$9/16 = 18/32$
$11/16 = 22/32$
$11/32 = 11/32$
$13/16 = 26/32$

The smallest wrench listed is $1/4$ inch. It is followed by: $5/16$, $11/32$, $3/8$, $1/2$, $9/16$, $11/16$, $3/4$, $13/16$, and $7/8$.

Point Standings

Race car circuits use formulas to rank drivers and cars over a season. The following point system was in place for IndyCar racing in 2011.

Points were awarded by place finish in each race. An extra two points were awarded to the driver who led the most laps in each race. Another point was given to the driver who won the **pole position**.

Finish	1st	2nd	3rd	4th	5th	6th	7th	8th	9th	10th	11th	12th	13th	14th	15th
Points	50	40	35	32	30	28	26	24	22	20	19	18	17	16	15

Finish	16th	17th	18th-24th	25th-on	Most laps led	Pole
Points	14	13	12	10	2	1

Dario Franchitti and Will Power were the top two IndyCar drivers in the 17-race 2011 season. Power won at Birmingham. He also had bonus points for the most laps led and pole position. How many points did he receive?

50 (1st finish points) + 2 (most laps led points) + 1 (pole point) = 53 points

Franchitti was twentieth at Loudon with the same bonus for laps led and pole position. How many points did he receive?

12 (18th-24th position points) + 2 (most laps led points) + 1 (pole point) = 15 points

The racers' points, by race, are given in the chart to the right. An "L" is for bonus points for most laps led. A "P" is for pole position. The Indianapolis 500 and the Twin Fort Worth races have different values than the standard formula.

Dario Franchitti earned 573 points. Will Power earned 555. Franchitti won the point title. The point system in place rewarded Franchitti's consistency. He won fewer poles and fewer races. He led more laps, finished more races, and had a better average finish.

Dario Franchitti gets ready for a race at the Milwaukee Mile track on June 19, 2011.

Franchitti Finish	Franchitti Points	Race Site	Power Finish	Power Points
1-L	52	St. Petersburg	2-P	41
3	35	Birmingham	1-L-P	53
3	35	Long Beach	10-P	21
4	32	Sao Paulo	1-L-P	53
12	24	Indianapolis	14	26
1	27	Fort Worth	3	18
7	13	Fort Worth	1	27
1-L-P	53	Milwaukee	4	32
5-L	32	Iowa	21	12
1	50	Toronto	24-L-P	15
3	35	Edmonton	1-L	52
2	40	Mid-Ohio	14	16
20-L-P	15	Loudon	5	30
4	32	Sonoma	1-L-P	53
4	32	Baltimore	1-L-P	53
8	24	Motegi	2	40
2-L	42	Kentucky	19-P	13

Season Performance

Matt Kenseth, Dale Earnhardt Jr., and Greg Biffle opened the 2012 NASCAR Sprint Cup season by finishing 1–2–3 at the Daytona 500. As the season neared its midway point, the three drivers still had the top three spots in the season points standings.

The line graph shows the ups and downs of each driver through the first 16 races of the season. Each driver is listed by his finish from race to race.

Matt Kenseth (17) reaches the finish line ahead of Dale Earnhardt Jr. (88) and Greg Biffle (16) to win the 2012 Daytona 500 on February 28, 2012.

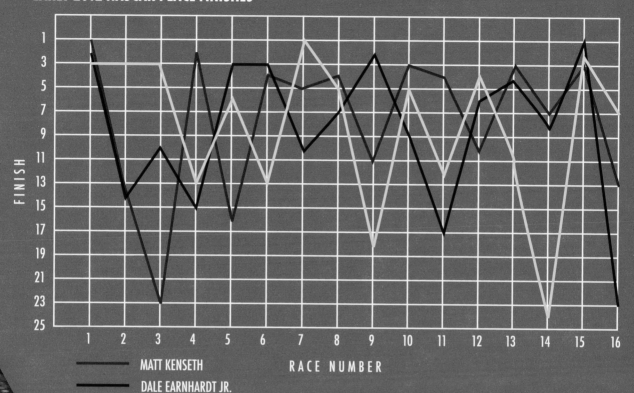

EARLY 2012 NASCAR PLACE FINISHES

FINISH

RACE NUMBER

——— MATT KENSETH
——— DALE EARNHARDT JR.
——— GREG BIFFLE

The Extra Mile

Miles per gallon (mpg) and mph are
two common **ratios** in auto racing.
Ratios compare one value to another.
Ratios can be expressed in different
ways. One way is a unit rate.

Race teams constantly check and
guess a car's fuel use. This helps them
decide the right time for pit stops. With
a chance to win late in the race, tough
choices must be made. A crew can
use precious seconds to refuel. Or the
crew can risk running out of fuel.

Two NASCAR crews think their
cars are getting 4.5 and 5.1 mpg.
Each car has a 17.75-gallon tank.
How many laps can each go on a
2-mile track before refueling?

First multiply the tank size by the mpg.

4.5 mpg x 17.75-gallon tank = 79.875 miles

The car getting 4.5 mpg can go 79.875 miles before refueling.

79.875 miles ÷ 2 (miles per lap) = 39.9 laps

The car can go almost 40 laps before stopping.

How far can the car getting 5.1 mpg go?

5.1 mpg x 17.75-gallon tank = 90.525 miles

The car getting 5.1 mpg can go 90.525 miles before refueling.

90.525 miles ÷ 2 (miles per lap) = 45.3

This car can go 45 laps before stopping.

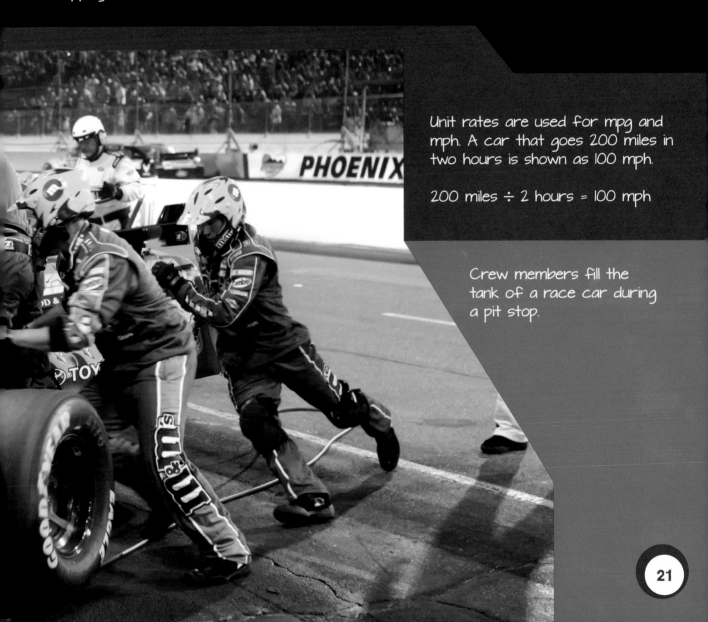

Unit rates are used for mpg and mph. A car that goes 200 miles in two hours is shown as 100 mph.

200 miles ÷ 2 hours = 100 mph

Crew members fill the tank of a race car during a pit stop.

Car Comparison

The sturdy cars used in NASCAR weigh approximately 3,400 pounds. The cars used for auto racing come in different sizes and shapes. Here is a table showing three major types of cars:

IndyCar rules aim to keep weight among cars as even as possible. Drivers who weigh less than 185 pounds have 4-pound or 9-pound plates added to their car until they reach the 185-pound mark.

SERIES	WEIGHT (IN POUNDS)	WHEEL BASE (IN INCHES)	GAS TANK (IN GALLONS)
Formula 1	1,360	124	Varies
IndyCar	1,565	118-121	18.5
NASCAR	3,400	110	18

Takuma Sato weighs 132 pounds. How could the weights be used to make Sato match 185 pounds?

185 - 132 = 53

Sato's team would have to add 53 pounds in weights.

5 x 9 (pound plates) = 45

2 x 4 (pound plates) = 8

45 + 8 = 53 pounds

The team has to add five 9-pound plates and two 4-pound plates.

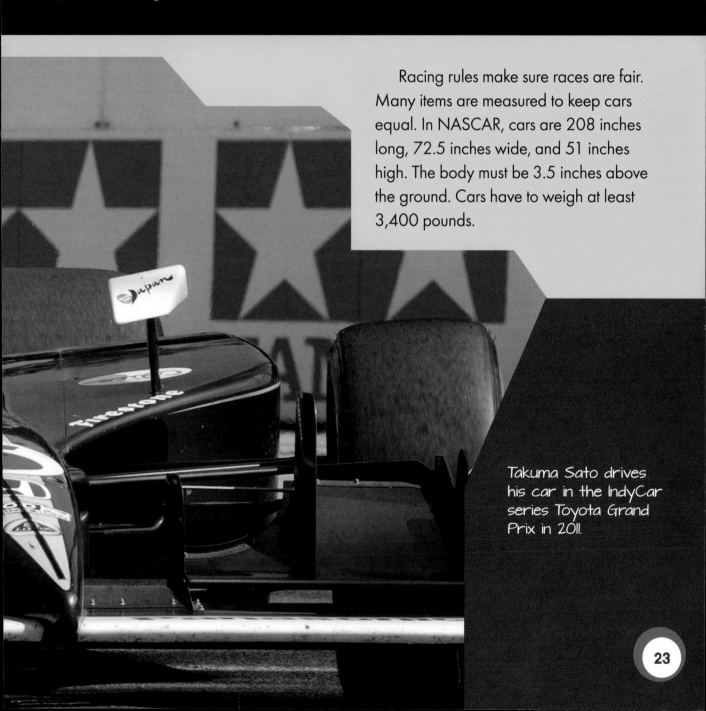

Racing rules make sure races are fair. Many items are measured to keep cars equal. In NASCAR, cars are 208 inches long, 72.5 inches wide, and 51 inches high. The body must be 3.5 inches above the ground. Cars have to weigh at least 3,400 pounds.

Takuma Sato drives his car in the IndyCar series Toyota Grand Prix in 2011.

Through the Years

Better technology lets race car speeds climb higher and higher. Going faster is not always better, though. Auto racing rules aim to keep speeds from going too high. That keeps drivers safe and it keeps the races fair.

The table below shows the winners' average speeds and the top qualifying speeds for each NASCAR Truck Series race at Daytona from 2000 through 2012.

Get a piece of paper to create a double-line graph. Use one line to track the changes in average speed for the winner. Use the other to track the speed of the top qualifier.

Allow for values from 110 to 190 mph in your graph. Plot the points. Connect the lines. Use your graph to help answer these questions.

- In how many years did both speeds go down? In how many years did both go up?
- What were the high points in speed for the winner and the top qualifier?
- What was the slowest winning speed? What was the slowest top qualifying speed?
- What is the only example of a speed going up or down for more than two years in a row?

In the 2001 and 2003 races, speeds went down from the previous year. In the 2002 and 2011 races, speeds went up. The top winning speed came at 146.6 mph in 2006. The best qualifying speed was 187.6 in 2000. The slowest winning speed came in 2004. The slowest qualifying leader was in 2008. The top qualifying speed went up in 2009, 2010, 2011, and 2012.

Year	Winner	Avg. Speed	Top Qualifying Speed
2000	Mike Wallace	130.2	187.6
2001	Joe Ruttman	129.4	186.1
2002	Robert Pressley	140.1	187.2
2003	Rick Crawford	127.6	182.9
2004	Carl Edwards	112.6	183.6
2005	Bobby Hamilton	124.9	182.5
2006	Mark Martin	146.6	178.6
2007	Jack Sprague	117.7	179.5
2008	Todd Bodine	127.6	176.5
2009	Todd Bodine	122.8	177.4
2010	Timothy Peters	115.3	177.5
2011	Michael Waltrip	130.0	179.0
2012	John King	119.2	181.5

Winning the Race

An extra fraction of a second at a pit stop can be the difference in an auto race. The cars are so close in speed that the slightest difference can have an impact on the race. One mph difference over the course of a race, one second saved in a pit stop, and one extra mpg are huge differences in a race.

Marco Andretti and Graham Rahal arrive at their pit stops at the same time. Andretti's crew finishes one second faster in a race when they are each averaging 150 mph. How much distance does a driver cover in one additional second at 150 mph?

NASCAR drivers Kevin Harvick and Mark Martin are in a 400-mile race. Harvick averages 140 mph. Martin averages 139 mph. How far ahead does Harvick finish?

$400 \div 140 = 2.85714$ hours of driving for Harvick

$400 \div 139 = 2.87770$ hours of driving for Martin

$2.85714 - 2.87770 = .02056$

Martin needs .02056 of an hour extra to finish the race.

There are 3,600 seconds in an hour.

$3,600 \times .02056 = 74.016$ seconds

Harvick would be 1 minute 14 seconds ahead.

Crew members for Marco Andretti service the car on a pit stop during the Indianapolis 500 on May 27, 2012.

Andretti would be 150 miles ahead in one hour.

150 ÷ 60 (minutes in an hour) = 2.5 miles

One minute would give Andretti a 2.5-mile advantage. To find how far he would go in a second, divide 2.5 miles by 60.

2.5 miles ÷ 60 (seconds in a minute) = .04167 miles

In one second, Andretti would be .04167 miles ahead. There are 5,280 feet in a mile.

5,280 x .04167 = 220

Andretti could use that one-second advantage leaving the pit to get a 220-foot advantage over Rahal.

1. IndyCar changed its rules about how much fuel cars could have in their tanks. It went from 22 gallons to 18.5 gallons between the 2011 and 2012 seasons. At an average of 3 mpg, how many fewer miles can an IndyCar go on a full tank of gas?

2. Tony Stewart's crew figures that he gets 4 mpg while racing. He gets 17 mpg while driving under a caution flag. He starts with 17.75 gallons. How much fuel does he have left after 30 miles of racing and 10 miles under a caution flag?

3. Spencer Massey reached 325.77 mph in a race. Massey beat Antron Brown, who went 320.43 mph. How many mph faster was Massey than Brown?

4. Ryan Newman averaged 142 mph for the first two hours of a 500-mile race. How many miles does he have left?

5. A race was reduced from 500 miles to 400 miles for 2012. The track is 2.5 miles long.
   A. How many laps were run in the 2012 race?
   B. How many laps fewer was that from previous seasons?

Answer Key

1. $22 - 18.5 = 3.5$
    $3 \times 3.5 = $ **10.5 miles**

2. 30 miles (racing) $\div$ 4 mpg $= 7.5$
    10 miles (caution flag) $\div$ 17 mpg $= 0.59$
    $7.5 + 0.59 = 8.09$ gallons
    $17.75 - 8.09 = $ **9.66 gallons**

3. $325.77 - 320.43 = $ **5.34 miles faster**

4. $142 \times 2 = 248$
    $500 - 248 = $ **252 miles**

5A. 400 miles total $\div$ 2.5 miles per lap $= $ **160 miles**

5B. 500 miles total $\div$ 2.5 miles per lap $= 200$
    $200 - 160 = $ **40 miles fewer**

Ryan Newman leads at the NASCAR Coca-Cola 600 at Charlotte Motorspeedway on May 27, 2012.

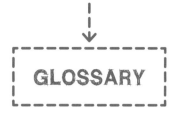
average (AV-uh-rij): An average is found by adding up a group of figures and then dividing the total by the number of figures added. Jimmie Johnson's average speed was 137.9 mph in the 2012 Brickyard 400.

backstretch (BAK-strech): A backstretch is the side opposite to the frontstretch on a racetrack. The backstretch at Daytona International Speedway is 3,000 feet.

denominator (di-NOM-uh-nay-tur): In fractions, the denominator is the number under the line that shows how many equal parts the whole number can be divided into. The denominator is the number at the bottom of a fraction.

frontstretch (FRUNT-strech): The frontstretch is the part of a racetrack where the start/finish line is located. The frontstretch of Daytona International Speedway is 3,800 feet.

intermediate (in-tur-MEE-dee-it): An intermediate racetrack is longer than 1 mile and up to 2 miles long. Atlanta Motor Speedway is an intermediate racetrack.

numerator (NOO-muh-ray-tur): In fractions, a numerator is the number above the line that shows how many parts of the whole are taken. A numerator is the top number in a fraction.

organization (or-guh-nuh-ZAY-shun): An organization is a number of people joined together for a certain purpose. NASCAR is by far the largest stock car racing organization in the world.

pole position (POHL puh-ZISH-uhn): Pole position is the first car at the start of a race. A car wins pole position by having the fastest qualifying lap.

qualifying (KWAHL-uh-fye-ing): A qualifying level is process in which drivers make a lap around the track to determine their starting position in a race. Ryan Newman averaged 194.2 miles per hour for a qualifying lap.

ratios (RAY-shee-ohz): Ratios are comparisons of two numbers, usually shown as fractions. Mpg and mph are two common ratios in auto racing.

straightaway (STRAY-tuh-way): A straightaway is the straight part of a racetrack. Drag racing is one quick burst down a straightaway.

LEARN MORE

Books

Arroyo, Sheri L. *How Race Car Drivers Use Math*. New York: Chelsea Clubhouse, 2010.

Gregorich, Barbara, and Christopher Jennison. *Racing Math: Checkered Flag Activities and Projects for Grades 4–8*. Tucson, AZ: Good Year Books, 2006.

Mahaney, Ian F. *The Math of NASCAR*. New York: PowerKids Press, 2012.

Web Sites

Visit our Web site for links about auto racing math:
childsworld.com/links

Note to Parents, Teachers, and Librarians: We routinely verify our Web links to make sure they are safe and active sites. So encourage your readers to check them out!

INDEX